THIS BOOK BELONGS TO:

KT-381-774

Brimming with creative inspiration, how-to projects, and useful information to enrich your everyday life, Quarto Knows is a favorite destination for those pursuing their interests and passions. Visit our site and dig deeper with our books into your area of interest: Quarto Creates, Quarto Cooks, Quarto Homes, Quarto Lives, Quarto Drives, Quarto Explores, Quarto Gifts, or Quarto Kids.

First published in French as
Dictionnaire des bonnes manières pour enfants and
Dictionnaire des grosses bêtises
© Larousse 2014, 2016

Published in English in 2018 by Walter Foster Jr.,
an imprint of The Quarto Group.
6 Orchard Road, Suite 100, Lake Forest, CA 92630, USA.
T (949) 380-7510 **F** (949) 380-7575 **www.QuartoKnows.com**

Walter Foster Jr. titles are also available at discount for retail, wholesale, promotional, and bulk purchase. For details, contact the Special Sales Manager by email at specialsales@quarto.com or by mail at The Quarto Group, Attn: Special Sales Manager, 401 Second Avenue North, Suite 310, Minneapolis, MN 55401 USA.

ISBN: 978-1-63322-524-4

Illustrated by Philippe Jalbert
Translated by Juliet Lecouffe

Printed in China
10 9 8 7 6 5 4 3 2 1

The Giggly Guide of How to Behave

Illustrated by Philippe Jalbert

It's polite to knock before entering someone's room.

Before you borrow something, ask if it's okay.

OOF!
OOF!

You shouldn't snoop around in other people's things.

Make sure to look others in the eye when talking to them.

If you borrow something from a friend, be sure to take good care of it.

You should always cover your mouth when you sneeze!

Everyone burps.
But it's polite to cover
your mouth and say,
"Excuse me!"
when you do.

Try not to bite off
more than you
can chew.

Don't speak with
your mouth full.

Even if you don't like your food, it's rude to spit it out.

It is polite to open doors for others.

Offering to help others is always the kind thing to do.

It's not nice to take others' things without asking.

You shouldn't pick your nose.

You should always wait patiently until it is your turn.

It's good manners
to say "Please"
when you ask for
something you want.

When you don't want something, say "No, thank you."

Look both ways
before crossing
the street.

Don't run with your mouth full.

Playing games with the driver is never a good idea.

And the car is not
a good place for
hide-and-seek either.

You should always keep your seatbelt buckled in a moving car.

Until you know how
to drive, don't play
with car keys.

It's never a good idea to cut your friends' hair.

Don't stand too close
to a lawnmower.

Curtains are not meant for wiping your hands or face.

You should always close the freezer door behind you.

It's never smart to tinker with tools or the plumbing.

Turning your sink into a swimming hole is not a good plan.

Be sure to turn the faucets off when you're done using them.

Don't put a whole bottle of bubble bath into the tub at once.

You should never
play with matches.

Knives belong
in the kitchen,
not the playroom.

Playing with makeup is a messy way to get into trouble.

Don't steal
from others.

You shouldn't
pee in the pool.

Playing near the pool's edge is dangerous business.

If you stick your finger in an electrical socket, you are sure to get a shocking surprise.

Always ask
permission before
redecorating
the house.

Bouncing on the bed can lead to unfortunate consequences.

CRACK!

It's best not to lean back in your chair.

When using public transportation, offer your seat to someone who needs it more.

Don't scratch your
butt in front of others.

Give yourself some space when you need to fart.